15 minute Azure Installation

Set up the Microsoft Cloud Server

by the Numbers

By BARRETT LEIBE

ISBN: 1508409609
ISBN-13: 978-1508409601

First Printing February 9, 2015

DEDICATION

This book is dedicated to all those who tried to evaluate the Azure Cloud Server System and failed. There are numerous comments of finding a block and giving up. I successfully overcame all the blocks and got it going. Now they can do it too.

CONTENTS

ACKNOWLEDGMENTS

Thanks to God for the ability to understand and communicate.
Thanks to my parents for teaching self-reliance and confidence.
Thanks to customers for keeping me going all these years.
Thanks to Keith Mayer of Microsoft for showing the way to getting this thing going. Without his blog entry this book could not have been written.

http://blogs.technet.com/b/keithmayer/archive/2013/09/0
4/step-by-step-remote-desktop-services-on-windows-
azure-a-cost-effective-alternative-to-desktop-as-a-service-
part-2.aspx

Thanks to you for buying this book.

CHAPTER 1 INTRODUCTION AND HISTORY

Congratulations!

You are on the verge of saving more than half the cost of a multi-user computer system using the cloud based Azure Server.

This book was written to save you forty hours of trial-and-error, searching internet weblogs and poorly written instructions. You also don't need to buy a $60. books written for those who have already spent $10,000 on the equivalent of a college education. By getting up and running before the thirty day trial period expires, you can quickly see if this system works for you.

On-line systems are nothing new. What makes Azure special is that you can use the same operating system and programs that you use in-house with no customization. Since the internet and world wide web became ubiquitous, programs have been written for the Linux operating system but you could not run the most popular ones. Amazon and Rackspace were first to offer the Microsoft Server on line and now Microsoft joins them. All three have concentrated efforts on hosting web sites and the Exchange email system for custom programming. But now, a breakthrough; you can easily install regular server software on the server and access it with a PC, tablet, or smart phone instead of establishing a more complex VPN (virtual private network). Microsoft decided to allow more than 2 users in April 2013 to use this Remote Desktop system. This gives you a direct replacement for an in-house system for less than half the cost. Although Citrix offered the same ability years ago, the price was high.

These same instructions work with the Amazon EC2 and Rackspace Server 2012 R2 and 2008.

What Can You Do With It?

Replace a hardware in-house server is the most obvious use. Now, it is thought of useful for large business but the benefit will mostly fe found by small companies without on-staff technologists. Let Microsoft do the maintenance! Because business owners are slow to accept the radical change, they are finding the HotServer, as a backup, worth the cost. Azure, with the FTP updating can be a low cost alternative to the many cloud backup products on the market.

What is It?

Microsoft Windows Azure is an on-line hosted computer. It features many physical computers with the latest Microsoft Windows Server 2012 R2 installed as virtual machines. There can be many copies of the virtual machine on each hardware computer and many virtual hard disk drives.

You can create these Virtual Machines and operate them just as you can your own hardware computer with the Server software installed.

Sign up for a free trial at www.azure.microsoft.com for 30 days but without this book, it might take you that long to get it going. Keep in mind that Microsoft charges for data out only so a geo-located server (a second location kept synchronized) may be costly because data leaves one server for the other. Start with the smallest power you need and increase it if you see the need.

History

In 1960, IBM and NCR developed the mainframe computer that many workstation terminals could access at one time and work with a single database. 1970 brought challengers with mini-computers reducing the cost by 90%, from DEC, Data General, Prime, and others. 1977 saw the micro computer (PC) drop that cost by another 90% and put a computer on every desktop. Still, the mini-computers were king in multi-user and on-line time share connection until the client-server paradigm developed. The access speed was a roaring 1200 baud (120 characters per second), enough for data entry. We sold and operated a time share system using an Alpha Micro mini-computer in 1980. The first client-server network systems appeared in 1982 and the Ethernet standard in 1984. Speeds are still increasing.

CHAPTER 2 DISADVANTAGES AND ADVANTAGES

Drawbacks

There are several drawbacks to this system rather than having your own hardware.

Your data is located out of the house. Although you may trust Microsoft not to peek or use it, there is always that possibility. Many sensitive organizations will not use the system for that reason, but it makes little difference to a shoe store, for example. And, the data can be encrypted before it leaves your premises. Of course, the data is encrypted during communication with the server. Most data breeches happen in house so on line can be safer.

The system depends on the internet being available. But, let's be serious. If the internet is down so is your business, anyway. Many companies have an alternate internet connection available, just in case. You can always go down to Wal-Mart and buy a wireless connection for $60. You can also work from McDonalds or the library. The same goes for your telephone system.

Microsoft's hardware may break or they may go bankrupt. Fat chance! The huge server farms are spread all over the globe and you can elect for a fail-over server in another location.

Benefits

You know the advantages. Expert 24/7 maintenance is included. Backup and fail-over and remote location assure security. The latest enterprise server version with automatic updates. Savings on hardware, facilities, power, rent, air conditioning, insurance. Remote access from anywhere. All of these factors add up to less than half the in-house cost.

You can install in 15 minutes, but please take all the time you need. If you get confused, let us know where so we can make it more plain.

Three Setup Plans

The first example is a simple single server. There are no licenses required and there can be many users but the limitation is two users at the same time. If a third logs on, he can ask that one of the others be logged off.

The second example is a single server that requires user licenses be purchased and installed. The limit is 24 users at the same time but more servers can be added for more users. There is a 90 day grace period before you have to purchase the licenses. Note that we see the licenses as a Microsoft reseller.

The third example sets up two servers; one for user control and one for the users' programs. This will allow a faster system for many users because you may find the single server system to be too slow.

CHAPTER 3 BEGIN THE INSTALLATION – SIMPLE SINGLE SERVER

1. You can begin in a browser later than Microsoft Internet Explorer 7, but need it to log on for the first time.

2. Go to www.windowsazure.com.

3. Select **Free Trial** select **Try it now** for 30 day $200 credit.

4. Sign in with your Microsoft account (was "live account").

   if you don't have an account, click to sign up for one - a credit card is necessary.

5. Enter your phone number to be called or texted price info.

6. Click **Agree** – Microsoft will call you with a code number.

7. You enter the code number and a billing form appears.

8. Enter credit card number – click **Agree** – click **Sign up.**

9. Click **Portal** – You are now shown the 30-second tour.

10. You are now signed in to the Portal.

   http://manage.windowsazure.com/

   *If you are not at "the choice of things to click on", click **NEW** at the bottom left of the screen*

   (write down the passwords and user names)

11. On the command bar, click **New**.

12. Click **Virtual Machine**, and then click **From Gallery**.

13. From **Choose an Image**, select an image from one of the lists. *The available images may differ depending on the subscription you're using.*

For example, click **Windows Server 2012 R2 Datacenter.** *This one is the most complete and costs the same as the others.*

14. Click the **arrow** to continue.

15. If multiple versions of the image are available, in **Version Release Date**, pick the version you want to use.

16. In **Virtual Machine Name**, type the name that you want to use for the virtual machine. For this virtual machine, type **MyTestVM1**.

    user   **MyTestVM1Admin**   password   **Mabc1234**

17. In **Tier**, select **Basic** instead of Standard to get the smallest size.

18. In **Size**, select the size of the virtual machine. The size you should select depends on the number of cores required to run your application. For this virtual machine, choose **A0** for the least price.

19. In **New User Name**, type a name for the administrative account that you want to use to manage the server. For this virtual machine, type **MyTestVM1Admin**.

    user   **VM1Admin**   password   **Mabc1234**

20. In **New Password**, type a strong password for the administrative account on the virtual machine. In **Confirm Password**, retype the password. Click the **arrow** to continue.

21. Select **Create a new cloud service**.

22. In **Cloud Service DNS Name**, type a name that uses between 3 and 24 lowercase letters and numbers. This name becomes part of the URI that is used to contact the virtual machine through the cloud service. For this virtual machine, type **MyService1**.

23. In **Region/Affinity Group/Virtual Network**, select where you want to locate the virtual machine.

   For example: **West US** *Select West if you will have only one Virtual Machine because Microsoft will do maintenance Friday after 5 pm; it will be later on the East coast.*

24. You can select a storage account where the VHD file is stored. For this tutorial, accept the default setting of **Use an Automatically Generated Storage Account**.

25. Under **Availability Set**, use the default setting of **None**. Click the arrow to continue.

26. Click the arrow to continue.

27. Check **Microsoft Antimalware** as you Security Extension. *There is no cost.*

28. Click the check mark to continue.

29. You are now back to the Portal with Virtual Machines selected.

30. Your virtual machine is starting – see the wobbly green bars at the bottom right of the screen.

31. Wait for the finish – then click the Virtual Machine **MyTestVM1.**

32. A help screen is shown – at the top, click **Endpoints.**

33. Click ADD at the bottom of the screen – Click the right Arrow.

34. Enter Name: select FTP - click the Check to accept the number and finish.

35. Do the same for HTTP and HTTPS.

36. Click Finish to End.

CHAPTER 4 LOG ON TO THE VIRTUAL MACHINE

You are in the Dashboard Screen.

You will need a Browser later than Internet Explorer 7 to log on for the first time.

1. On the command bar at the bottom of the screen of the Dashboard, click **Connect**.

2. You are asked to save a file, **MyTestVM1.rdp**. do so. This becomes your connection file for the future. Make an icon to click on it for your desktop.

   To make the icon, right-click your desktop, click New, click Shortcut, and browse to the file. Double-click it to create the icon.

3. You may now Sign out by clicking your email address at the top right of the screen to close the browser window.

4. Go to the location of the file you saved, **MyTestVM1.rdp**, and double-click it. In the password box, type the user name (MyTestVM1Admin) and password (Mabc1234) that you specified when you created the virtual machine and then click **OK**. *You may not log on with a computer using Windows XP until a following setting.*

5. You log in to the server by double-clicking the desktop icon, **MyTestVM1.rdp**

   The properties for the icon are:

   full address: **VM1Admin**.cloudapp.net:xxxxx

   where xxxxx is the instance address from the installation

   prompt for credentials:i:1

Alternatively you can type in:

Start -> mstsc.exe -> **VM1Admin**.cloudapp.net:xxxxx

This opens the virtual machine with the Server Manager Dashboard in view.

6. Click **Yes** on the right to find your local printer.

If the server window does not fill your workstation screen, you can set the size.

7. Click **Local Server** on the left list.

8. Click **On** on the right side of **IE Enhanced Security Configuration** to click both **OFF.**

9. Download and install **Java** from the web site **www.Java.com.**

   This will let you use the browser for general use.

10. Click** Manage **at the top right of the Server Manager Screen.

11. Click **Server Manager Properties.**

12. Check **Do not start** to prevent startup on logon.

CHAPTER 5 ADD USERS

1. Click the **Start** icon at the bottom left of the screen. *You can also use the Start key.*

2. Click **Control Panel** -> **User Accounts** -> **Change account type** -> **Add a user account.**

3. Enter a new User Name and Password for each user.

4. Click one of the names to be able to change the account type to Administrator, if required.

5. Close the user window.

6. Open the **Server Manager.**

7. Click the second icon from the left at the bottom of the screen.

8. Click **Local Server** in the vertical list on the left.

the **Properties** screen appears.

9. click **Enabled** just to the right of "Remote Desktop".

10. click to remove check from the box at "Allow connections only from computers running Remote Desktop with Network Level Authentication [recommended]".

This is to allow logging on from a computer without this capability, such as XP Home. You can click it later if all your workstations have it. You can find out if your workstation has it by trying it.

11. Click **Select Users** on this **System Properties** window.

12. Click **Add.**

13. Type in the name of a user and click **Check Names** – click **OK.**

14. Do this for VM1Admin and Guest.

15. Do it again for each user -> click **OK** -> click **OK** to close the "System Properties" window

16. Click the **Time** display at the bottom right of the screen.

17. Click to change date, time, and zone settings.

18. Close the **Server Manager** window by clicking the red **X** at the top right of the screen.

CHAPTER 6 ADD A PROGRAM TO THE SERVER FROM YOUR WORKSTATION

You are now ready to install application programs. The server and its management are the same as one installed in your office. The books and documentation are the same.

Please remember to NOT place data files in the **Program Files** directory or the **Program Files (x86)** directory. This may cause entries to be delayed.

Set Share for at the application directory for each user.

1. Right-click the directory

2. Click Share

3. Click Advanced Sharing

4. Type in each user

5. Click Read/Write

6. Click the **Files** icon at the bottom left of the screen - it is the fourth from the left, tan colored

7. Double-click **Local Disk (C:)** under **Computer** in the list

8. From your Workstation, you can copy the program or files you need and paste them to the Server and then install as usual

9. If you program is on a CD, copy the entire CD to the server drive and install it from there

10. double-click your program to set it up and begin using it

CHAPTER 7 ADD A PRINTER

How to use your local printer on the Azure Virtual Machine:

Microsoft includes a component called Easy-Print. Your networked local printers should be automatically available to print to from the cloud server. Make sure the client computer has the printer driver installed. If it is using Windows XP, you may need the Service Pack 3 installed.

It may take a while for the printer to be seen, or the server needs to be restarted. In some cases, possibly with an older printer, it may not be seen from Azure. If so, try this:

1. In Windows Azure Virtual Machine open control panel.

2. Under Hardware click on **View devices and printers.**

3. Click on **Add a printer.**

4. Click on **The printer that I want isn't listed.**

5. Click **Add a local printer or network printer with manual settings**.

6. Click on **Next.**

7. In the **Use an existing port** select **Use an existing port**, not the default LPT1 (printer port) .

8. Click on the list drop and you will see lots of available ports - and your computer ports are listed too. You will see ports like TS001,   TS002,...

9. Choose TS001 port. TS stands for Terminal Services redirected printer.

10. Click **Next.**

11. Select your printer manufacturer and select the printer from the list.

If your printer is not on the list, click **Windows Update**

Wait a while for it to finish.

If you printer is not listed, it may not work.

This window confirms your selected printer name - you can change it.

12. Click **Next** - the printer driver installation starts.

The next screen offers you to share the printer. If it is shared, all virtual machines on your virtual network can print on that local printer. Share it and click on Next.

The printer must be turned on and on your network or local computer.

13. Select Pooling and choose 2 or 3 TS ports to make sure one works.

14. You are done! Print a test page.

The printing may be relative slow. You might get a message that Printer is not responding. But wait, it is going to print. *You can set the priority of each printer.*

To add another printer of the same type, turn off the first one and go through the instructions for the second one. Give it a different name.

If you re-boot the server, you will have to enter the printer information again.

CHAPTER 8 ALLOW MORE THAN TWO USERS AT THE SAME TIME

You receive two free access licenses. For more users they must be purchased before the trial period of 120 days expires. We rent these for $10 per month or you can use any other dealer. If you are a reseller, sign up for a Microsoft SPLA agreement with Synnex or another distributor.

If you log on a third user, the system will ask which of the other two to close. The following will remove this restriction, allowing up to 24 users. If your program is disk access, compute, or bandwidth intensive or needs more RAM, you would have to select a larger server size. It may be less costly to use two or more servers. Try it to find out.

If you want to allow more than two users, follow the instructions in Chapter 15 instead of Chapter 3. However, you can do the following:

Start the Server Manager by clicking the second icon from the left at the bottom of the screen.

1. Click **Add Roles and features.**

2. Click **Next.**

3. Click **Next** with Role-based or feature-based installation selected.

4. Click **Next** with your server highlighted.

5. The Server Roles list is shown.

6. Click **Application Server.**

7. Click **File and Storage Services.**

8. Click **Print and Document Services** and then click **Add Features** at the bottom.

9. Click **Remote Desktop Services.**

10. Click **Next** and the Features list is shown.

11. Click **.NET Framework 4.5.**

12. Click **BranchCache.**

13. Click **Group Policy Management.**

14. Click **Remote Server Administration Tools** and then click **Add Features.**

15. Click **Windows Server Backup.**

16. Click **Print and Document Service.**

17. Click **Print Server.**

18. Click **Next.**

19. Click to select **Restart the destination server automatically if required.**

20. Cclick **Install** and wait for completion.

21. Click **Close.**

22. Once again, click **Add Roles and features.**

23. Click **Next.**

24. Check **Remote Desktop Licensing** and then click **Add Features** at the bottom.

25. Click **Next.**   Click **Next.**   Click **Next.**

26. Check **Restart the destination server automatically if required** and click **Yes.**

27. Click **Remote Access** – and check **all three functions.**

28. Click **Install.**

Wait for the update to finish.

CHAPTER 9 ADD REMOTE DESKTOP LICENSES

2 are included free

1. Click **Start.**

2. Click **Administrative Tools.**

3. Double-click **Remote Desktop Services.**

4. Double-click **Remote Desktop Licensing Manager.**

5. Double-click name of server.

6. Click **Action -> Activate Server.**

7. Click **Next.**   Click **Next.**

8. Enter **name.**

9. Click **Next.**

10. Enter *Address.*

11. Click **Next.**   Click **Next.**

12. Choose **Service Provider License Agreement.**

13. Agreement Number 6992xxxx   (Standard Enrollment 6992xxxx).

   You get this number from a Microsoft reseller or directly from Microsoft Licensing.

   get information from Microsoft Call Center: (716)871-2781 / (888) 352-7140).

14. Product version: Windows Server 2012.

15. License type: RDS per user CAL.

16. Quantity: 1.

17. Close all windows by clicking on the red X at the top right.

CHAPTER 10 REFERENCE OF ALL SELECTIONS

If there is a problem with your installation, it might be a typing error. You can check that the correct checks are set as follows:

On Server Manager

1. At top right, click **Manage.**

2. Click **Add Roles and Features.**

3. Click **Next.**

4. Click **Role-based or features-based installation.**

5. Click **Next**, your Virtual Machine is shown.

6. Click **Next.**

7. Click **Application Server**, click check at **.NET Framwork 4.5.**

8. Click on **File and Storage Services.**

9. Click **Network Policy and Access Services**, click check at **Network Policy Server.**

10. Click **Print and Document Services**, click on **Print Server.**

11. Click **Remote Desktop Services.**

12. Check **Remote Desktop Connection Broker.**

13. Check **Remote Desktop Gateway.**

14. Check **Remote Desktop Licensing.**

15. Check **Remote Desktop Session Host.**

16. Check **Remote Desktop Web Access.**

17. Click **Volume Activation Service.**

18. Click **Web Server (IIS).**

19. Click **Web Server.**

20. Click **Common HTTP Features.**

21. Check **Default Document.**

22. Check **Directory Browsing.**

23. Check **HTTP Errors.**

24. Check **Static Content.**

25. Check **HTTP Redirection.**

26. Click **Health and Diagnostics.**

27. Check **HTTP Logging.**

28. Check **Logging Tools.**

29. Check **Request Monitor.**

30. Check **Tracing.**

31. Click **Performance.**

32. Check **Static Content Compression.**

33. Click **Security.**

34. Check **Request.**

35. Check **Basic Authentication.**

36. Check **Client Certificate Mapping-Authentication.**

37. Check **IP and Domain Restrictions.**

38. Check **Windows Authentication.**

39. Click **Application Development.**

40. Check **.NET Extensibility 4.5.**

41. Check **ASP NET 4.5.**

42. Check **ISAPI Extensions.**

43. Check **ISAPI Filters.**

44. Click **Management Tools.**

45. Check **IIS Management Console.**

46. Click **IIS 6 Management Compatibility.**

47. Check **IIS 6 Metabase Compatibility.**

48. Check **IIS 6 Management Console.**

49. Check **IIS Management Scripts and Tools.**

50. Click **Next.**

    then the Features list appears

51. Click **.NET Framework 4.5 Features.**

52. Check **.NET Framework 4.5.**

53. Check **ASP.NET 4.5.**

54. Click **WCF Services.**

55. Check **TCP Port Sharing.**

56. Check **BranchCache.**

57. Check **Group Policy Management.**

58. Check **IIS Hostable Web Core.**

59. Check **Media Foundation.**

60. Check **RAS Connection Manager Administration Kit.**

61. Click **Remote Server Administration Tools.**

62. Click **Feature Administration Tools.**

63. Check **SMTP Server Tools.**

64. Click **Role Administration Tools.**

65. Check **Remote Desktop Services Tools.**

66. Check **DHCP Server Tools.**

67. Click **File Services Tools.**

68. Check **DFS Management Tools.**

69. Check **File Server Resource Manager Tools.**

70. Check **Services for Network File System Manager.**

71. Check **Network Policy and Access Services Tools.**

72. Check **Print and Document Services Tools.**

73. Check **Volume Activation Tools.**

74. Check **RPC over HTTP Proxy.**

75. Check **SMB 1.0/CIFS File Sharing Support.**

76. Click **User Interfaces and Infrastructure.**

77. Check **Graphical Management Tools and Infrastructure.**

78. Check **Server Graphical Shell.**

79. Check **Windows Internal Database.**

80. Click **Windows PowerShell.**

81. Check **Windows PowerShell 4.0.**

82. Check **Windows PowerShell ISE.**

83. Check **Windows Server Backup.**

84. Check **WoW64 Support.**

85. Click **Remote Desktop Service.**

86. Click **Role Services.**

87. Check **Remote Desktop Gateway** - click **Add Features.**

88. Check **Remote Desktop Licensing** - click **Add Features.**

89. Check **Remote Desktop Web Access** - click **Add Features.**

90. Click **Next** , click **Next** , click **Next** , click **Next** , click **Next** .

91. Check **Restart the destination server automatically if required,** click **Yes.**

92. Click **Install** and wait until finished.

93. Click **Close.**

CHAPTER 11 ADD THE ABILITY TO SCAN

FROM A LOCAL SCANNER

If you use a program on the server that allows scanning of documents or photographs to the database. We offer a pair of programs that allow this to work. The scanner may be attached either by USB or on a local network. The fee is $99. per year. You may install and test the demo for 30 days before purchase.

FIRST download the **client** software and install on your workstation

SECOND download the **server** software from the server and install on the server

The cost of the license:	single user	10 users	unlimited
Monthly rental	10.	10./user	35.
Purchase	99.	180.	380.

If you need a program to display the document, you can install on the server: Adobe Reader or the Chrome browser.

http://get.adobe.com/reader/

www.google.com/chrome

You can rent server user licenses from us for $5. per month each. Just email the request.

CHAPTER 12 USE DUAL MONITOR SCREENS

This can be set up for two monitors or one notebook screen and one monitor. You simply need to add a line to the log on icon or statement.

The line is:

use multimon:i:1 instead of use multimon:i:0

If you are typing:

Start -> mstsc.exe -> **VM1Admin**.cloudapp.net:xxxxx

You can type in:

Start -> mstsc.exe/multimon -> **VM1Admin**.cloudapp.net:xxxxx

To log out of the Terminal Services session, click the **Start Button**

Click the **User Name** at the top right of the screen

Click **Sign out**

CHAPTER 13 SET UP A FTP SERVER

Set up the FTP server in Windows Azure Virtual Machine with FileZilla

You may want to set up the FTP server so that you can synchronize files from your local PC or server with the cloud server. This is useful to maintain a working server in the cloud in case of disaster or to use while on the road, or just as a backup.

We use the FileZilla server. You can access the files from a PC using the FileZilla client, a browser, or some other FTP client program.

You can automate the synchronization or upload using the WinSCP client program. It will be started by the Scheduler program on your PC.

With a FTP server on the Virtual Machine and a FTP client on your PC, you can copy files to and from the Virtual Machine. You can also do this with Windows Explorer, but FTP can be automated.

1. If you haven't done so already, open the management portal,

http://manage.windowsazure.com and click on the VM dashboard

2. Make a note of your **Public virtual IP (VIP) address.**

3. Add an endpoint labeled **ftp**, Protocol **TCP**, public port **21**, private port **21.**

4. Add another endpoint labeled labeled **ftp2**, Protocol **TCP**, public port **50001**, private port **50001** *wait for it to finish.*

5. Add another endpoint labeled labeled **ftp3**, Protocol **TCP**, public port **50000**, private port **50000** *wait for it to finish.*

6. Add another endpoint labeled labeled **ftp4**, Protocol **TCP**, public port **14147**, private port **14147** *wait for it to finish.*

7. Log on to the virtual machine and start the Internet Explorer.

8. Download the FTP server from https://filezilla-project.org and install it. *Be sure to decline the two extra program offers.*

9. Start the FileZilla server to see the FileZilla Interface.

10. For the **Administration password** use your same one for the VM.

11. For the Port use **50000.**

12. Click **Always connect to this server** if you want to startup automatically.

13. Click **OK.**

14. Click **Edit.**

15. Click **Groups.**

16. Click **Add.**

17. Type in **group1.**

18. Check **Enable access for users inside group.**

19. **Bypass user lmit of server.**

20. Click **OK.**

21. Click **Edit.**

22. Click **Users.**

23. Click **Add.**

24. Type in the name of the administrator.

25. Click **OK.**

26. Check **Enable account.**

27. Check **Password.**

28. Type in the **Password** for that user, the administrator.

29. Click **Shared folders.**

30. Click **Add.**

31. Click **Local Disk (C:)** or any folder you wish to use.

be sure this folder and the drive and directories it is on are all shared with permissions for Everyone.

32. Check all **Files** blocks.

33. Check all **Directories** blocks.

34. Click **Set as home dir.**

35. Click **OK** to go back to the FileZilla Interface.

36. Click **Edit.**

37. Click **Settings.**

38. Type **50001** to the **Listen on these ports:** field.

39. Click **Passive mode settings.**

40. Check **Use custom port range.**

41. Type in **50000** and **50001** or any range above 1000.

   (that you have set as VM endpoints)

42. Check **Use the following IP:**

43. Type in the URL given in your **Public virtual IP (VIP) address.**

   for example, (xxx.xxx.xx.xx it should appear automatically)

44. Unclick **Don't use external IP for local connections.**

45. **Click Security Settings.**

46. Unclick **Block incoming and outgoing.**

47. Click Admin Interface Settings.

48. Type in **50001** into **Port on which the admin interface should listen:**

49. Click **OK** to go back to the FileZilla Interface.

50. Click **C:** instead of **/C/** to show real file names.

51. Change the firewall:

52. Click the **Start** icon at the bottom left of the VM screen.

53. Type **Firewall** and it appears in a search field.

54. Click **Allow an app or feature through Windows Firewall.**

55. Click **Allow another app...**

56. Browse for **FileZilla Server.exe** in C:/Program Files (x86)/

  (not FileZilla Interface)

57. Click **Add.**

58. Check Network types...   **Private** and **Public.**

59. Click **OK.**

60. Click **Start** icon at bottom left of screen.

61. Click **Control Panel.**

62. Click View network status and tasks.

63. Click **Windows Firewall.**

64. Click **Advanced settings.**

65. Click **Inbound Rules.**

66. Be sure **FileZilla Server** is marked Profile **All**,

    Enabled **Yes,** Action **Allow**.

67. Click **Finish.**

68. lose this window by clicking the **red X.**

69. lose the **Windows Firewall** window by clicking the **red X.**

Now we are going to be sure the shares and permissions are set for the

folder we want to access with FTP.

70. Click the **Windows Explorer icon**,

    the beige file folder at the bottom of the screen.

71. Right-click **Local Disk (C:).**

72. Click **Properties.**

73. Click **Sharing.**

74. Click **Share.**

75. Click **Advanced Sharing.**

76. Check **Share this folder.**

77. Click **Permissions.**

78. Select **Group or user names Everyone.**

79. Check the Full Control box **Allow.**

80. Click **OK.**Click **OK.**   Click **Close.**

81. Double-click **Local Disk (C:).**

82. *Right-click the folder you selected for the FileZilla Share and do the same.*

83. Check that the server is working by typing in the URL to your browser.

ftp://<< *your Public virtual IP (VIP) address>>*:50001

You should see a list of files in the shared folder.

84. Install the FileZilla client program and use that IP for the host, and 50001 for the port with your user name and password.

You should see a list of files in the shared folder.

If later you cannot open the Edit function, change the FileZilla Server Interface.xml file entry.

<Item name="Start Minimized" type="numeric">1</Item>

     to

<Item name="Start Minimized" type="numeric">0</Item>

CHAPTER 14 AUTOMATE THE FTP SYNCHRONIZATION FROM YOUR PC TO THE CLOUD SERVER

1. Install the FTP client WinSCP on the PC to automate the synchronization.

2. Download the program from the web site:

   http://winscp.net/download/winscp554setup.exe

   Be sure to skip the extra programs they try to sell you.

3. The program WinSCP.exe installs in your program directory WinSCP

4. Go there and try the program by typing WinSCP.exe

5. To automate, you have two choices, a single .bat file or a .bat file with a text file list of commands. Please either of these in your C:\ directory.

The word "remote" copies from your PC to the server. "local" goes the other way, and "both" synchronizes both.

Remember if data files are open they will not back up correctly.

The single file is:

@echo off

cd c:\program files (x86)\winscp

winscp.com /command "option batch abort" "option confirm off" "open ftp://user:Userit3@ example.com:50001" "synchronize remote c:\examplefile.txt /" "exit"

or:

```
@echo off

cd c:\Program Files (x86)\WinSCP

winscp.com /command "option batch abort" "option confirm off" "open
ftp://user@example.com/" "put examplefile.txt /home/user/" "exit"
```

The two file couple is:

The first file named "winftp.bat" is:

```
@echo off

winscp.com /winftp.txt
```

And the second file named "winftp.txt" is:

```
option batch abort

option confirm off

open ftp://user:password@example.com:50001/

put c:\files\*.* /home/user/

close

exit
```

CHAPTER 15 BEGIN THE INSTALLATION –

SINGLE SERVER FOR LICENSES

Set up of a Microsoft Windows Server 2012 R2 in the cloud.

This setup will use one virtual server for an Active Directory Domain Controller and DNS server, and also configured as a Remote Desktop Session Host, Web Access gateway, and Connection Broker. The first is dedicated to authorizing users and checking their log in and user management. The second is where the user programs and data reside. The server can support up to 26 users at the same time. You can add servers for more users.

Microsoft charges a small monthly fee and for each user license more than two plus data transfer out of the server. If you set up a server without Active Directory, you get two licenses free.

We will:

      A. Prepare the Infrastructure.

      B. Register a DNS Server in Windows Azure.

      C. Define a Virtual Network in Windows Azure.

      D. Configure Windows Server Active Directory in a Windows Azure VM

      E. Configure Remote Desktop Session Virtualization in the Windows Azure VM .

      F. Install user licenses.

      G. Connect to Remote Desktop on the Internet.

Estimated time to complete: 2 hours.

A: Prepare the Infrastructure

1.   Login to the Windows Azure Management Portal.

Login to the web-based Windows Azure Management Portal at http//manage.windowsazure.com.

On the blue side navigation bar at the left side, there are the options for managing Virtual Machines, Virtual Networks, Storage and Settings. You can scroll down to see all options.

2. Make a new Affinity Group.

Affinity groups group your cloud-based services together, such as Virtual Machines, Virtual Networks and Storage. Azure will keep all group services within the same data center.

a.   Select Settings from the blue side bar in the Windows Azure Management Portal.

b.   On the Settings page, select the Affinity Groups tab on the top navigation bar.

c.   Click the +ADD button on the bottom navigation bar.

d.   On the Create Affinity Group form, enter Name: Enter a unique name for your new Affinity Group, such as XXXvma01 (use your initials for XXX)

Region: Select the "South Central US" datacenter sub-region. Click the Check button to continue.

3. Make a new Storage Account.

a.   Click the +NEW button on the bottom toolbar in the Management Portal and select Data Services -> Storage -> Quick Create.

b.   Enter a unique name for your new storage account URL, such as XXXtestor01 (use your initials for XXX)

c.   Region/Affinity Group: Select the Affinity Group you created above.

d.   Geo-Replication is enabled. Your outgoing data flow will be doubled and increase cost, but it is usually worth it. Each site keeps three copies of your data.

e.   Click the CREATE STORAGE ACCOUNT check button to continue.

B: Register a DNS Server

Set the internal IP address to use for Active Directory-integrated Dynamic DNS services.

1. You are in the Management Portal.

2. Select Networks on the blue side panel.

3. Click the +NEW button located on the bottom bar and select Network Services -> Virtual Network -> Register DNS Server.

4. Enter the DNS Server Name: XXXtestdns01 and DNS Server IP Address: 10.0.0.4

5. Click the REGISTER DNS SERVER check button.

C: Create a Virtual Network

The virtual network supports Active Directory, Database and SharePoint virtual machines

1.   You are in the Management Portal.

2.   Select Networks on the blue side panel.

3.   Click the +NEW button located on the bottom bar and select Network Services -> Virtual Network -> Quick Create.

4.   Enter the Virtual Network Name: XXXtestnet01 and Address Space: 10.---.---.--- and

Maximum VM Count: 4096 [CIDR: /20].

5.   For Location, select South Central US.

6.   For Affinity Group, Select the Affinity Group XXXvma01 created in A.2.d. above.

7.   For DNS Server, Select XXXtestdns01 created in B.4. above.

8.   Click the CREATE A VIRTUAL NETWORK check button to finish.

D. Create an Active Directory in a Virtual Machine (VM)

Create a new Virtual Machine (VM) to run the Active Directory domain controller in a new Active Directory Forest.

1.　You are in the Management Portal.

2.　Select Virtual Machines on the blue side panel.

3.　Click the +NEW button located on the bottom bar and select Compute -> Virtual Machines -> from the Gallery.

4.　Select the Windows Server 2012 Datacenter from the selection list.

5.　Click the right-arrow button.

6.　On the Configuration page, type the Virtual Machine Name: XXXtestor01.

7.　Select Tier Basic for Size A0.

8.　Enter a new Local Administrator User Name: vadmin and Password: Pp123456.

9.　Click the Right Arrow button to continue.

10.　You are in the Virtual Machine Configuration page.

11.　Accept Create a new cloud service.

12.　Accept the DNS Name: XXXtestor01.cloudapp.net

13.　Enter Region/Affinity Group/Virtual Network: XXXtestnet01 – that created in C.4 above.

14.　For the Virtual Network Subnets, Accept: Subnet-1 (10.0.0.0/23)

15.　For the Storage Account, select: XXXtestor01 – that created in A.3.b above.

16. For the Availability Set, create one name: XXXtestad

17. Click the Right Arrow button to continue.

18. Include this endpoint:

       b. HTTPS endpoint

     1. Protocol = TCP

     2. Public Port = 443

     3. Private Port = 443

19. Click the Right Arrow button to continue.

20. You are still in the Virtual Machine Configuration page.

21. Accept the check, Install the VM Agent.

22. Click the Microsoft Antimalware box.

23. Click the check button to continue.

24. You are in the Management Portal. Wait a few minutes until the status of the Virtual Machine, named XXXtestor01, shows *running*. (And, the green squiggly stops at the bottom right corner).

25. Click on the name of the new Virtual Machine, XXXtestor01.

26. Click Dashboard.

27. You are in the Dashboard Page.

28. The Internal IP Address shown on the right side of the page should be 10.0.0.4

If it is not, click the Delete button at the bottom of the page and start again with Instruction B: above.

29. Click the Attach button on the bottom toolbar and select Attach Empty Disk.

30. Accept the file name: XXXtestor01-XXXXXX or enter: XXXtestor01-data01

31. Enter the size: 10 for 10 GB

32. Accept the Host Cache Preference: None

33. Click the Check button to continue.

34. You are in the Dashboard Page.

35. Click the Connect button located on the bottom toolbar.

36. Click Open to launch a Remote Desktop Connection to the virtual machine.

37. Enter the user name: vadmin, and password: Pp123456 selected in D.7. above.

38. You are in the Virtual Machine desktop page with the Server Manager Dashboard screen showing.

39. Do not search for printers, etc. as asked.

40. Click Local Server.

41. Click remote desktop.

42. Unclick Allow connections only from computers …

43. This will allow log on from other than computers with Windows 7 and above.

44. Click OK.

45. Click the time icon at the bottom right and set the time zone.

46. Click File and Storage Services -> Disks -> Tasks, to start the new volume wizard.

This creates a new partition on the additional data disk attached above in D.24 and format this partition as a new F: NTFS volume. This volume will be used for NTDS DIT database, log and SYS VOL folder locations.

47. Click Next.

48. Click Disk 2.

49. Click Next.

50. Click OK.

51. Click Next.

52. Accept Drive Letter F:.

53. Click Next.

54. Click Next.

55. Click Create.

56. Check Cloxe.

57. Click the upper left square to return to the Server Manager Dashboard.

58. Click Add Roles and Features.

59. Click Next.

60. Click Server Roles.

61. Click Roles.

62. Click Role-based.

63. Click Select.

64. Click install Active Directory Domain Services

65. Click promote this server to a domain controller in a new forest.

66. Enter Active Directory Forest name: contoso.com   (root domain name)

   CONTOSO.COM is a Microsoft server.

67. Accept the Volume Location for NTDS database, log and SYSVOL folders: F:

Wait a few minutes for the Active Directory to be installed.

68. Restart the virtual machine by clicking Start -> admin -> restart

Wait a few minutes for the restart.

We now have finished the Active Directory Virtual Machine that will authenticate all users to the system. We can use this VM for up to 25 users or add additional VMs for 25 users each.

E: Configure Remote Desktop Session Virtualization

This uses the same Virtual Machine to run Remote Desktop Sessions. It can be faster to use one VM for Active Directory and one or more for user sessions, but more expensive. If you want to run both sessions on one VM, keep that name, XXXtestor01 for the following.

54. Click on the name of the new Virtual Machine, XXXtestor01.

55. You are in the Dashboard Page.

56. Click the Connect button located on the bottom toolbar.

57. Click Open to launch a Remote Desktop Connection to the virtual machine.

58. Enter the user name: contoso\admin, and password: Pp123456 selected in D.7. above.

   Note that you must use the contoso.

59. You are in the Virtual Machine desktop page with the Server Manager screen showing.

60. Click Local Server.

61. Click Remote management and make sure it is Enabled.

62. Click Dashboard.

63. Click Add roles and features.

64. Click the Next button on the Before you begin page.

65. Select Remote Desktop Services installation on the Select installation type page.

66. Click the Next button.

67. Select Quick Start.

68. Click Next.

69. Select Session based desktop deployment

70. Click Next.

71. The server XXXtestor01 is in the Selected listbox of the Select a server page

72. Click the Next button.

73. Check Restart the destination server automatically if required, on the Confirmation page.

74. Click Deploy.

75. Wait while the deployment is made. If the server does not reset itself, restart it in the browser Management Portal window.

76. You are in the Management Portal. Wait a few minutes until the status of the Virtual Machine, named XXXtestor01, shows *running*. (And, the green squiggly stops at the bottom right corner).

77. Click on the name of the new Virtual Machine, XXXtestor01.

78. You are in the Dashboard Page.

79. Click the Connect button located on the bottom toolbar.

80. Click Open to launch a Remote Desktop Connection to the virtual machine.

81. Enter the user name: contoso\admin, and password: Pp123456 selected in D.7. above.

   Note that you must use the contoso.

82. You are in the Virtual Machine desktop page with the Server Manager screen showing.

Add Users

1. Click the Start icon at the bottom left of the screen. *You can also use the Start key.*

2. Click Control Panel.

3. Click User Accounts.

4. Click Change account type.

5. Click the Advanced tab at the top.

6. Click Advanced.

7. The lusrmgr – Local Users and Groups screen is shown.

8. Click Action -> New User.

9. Type in the user name: U1.

10. Type in the password: Pp123456.

11. Type in the password again in Confirm password.

12. Click Create.

13. Enter another user, U2 with password, Pp123456.

14. Close the lusmgr screen by clicking the red X at the top right.

15. Close the User Accounts screen.

16. Close the Control Panel screen.

17. You are in the Server Manager Dashboard screen.

F. Install user licenses

You can buy the user SAL licenses several ways. For this case, we assume you have a key number from a SPLA dealer and the number is 1234567890.

1.   Click Remote Desktop Services.

Click servers.

The server XXXtestor01 is shown.

Right-Click the server XXXtestor01.

Click RD Licensing Manager.

Right-Click the server XXXtestor01 again that is shown as Not activated.

Click Activate Server.

Click Next.

Accept Automatic.

Click Next.

Fill out the form with name and company information.

Click Next.

Enter the optional information on the form.

Click Next.

You are shown that the server has been activated.

Click Next.

You may not enter the user licenses. (SAL)

Click Next.

The RD Licensing Manager screen is shown.

Click Action.

Click Install Licenses.

Click Next.

In the License Program drop down list, select Service Provider License Agreement.

Click Next.

Type in the agreement number. (1234567890)

Click Next.

On the Product Version drop down list, click Windows Server 2012.

On the License Type drop down list, click RDS Per User CAL.

For the number of licenses, type in 3.

Click Next.

You are show that the licenses are successfully installed.

Click Finish.

You are in the RD Licensing Manager screen.

There is a yellow triangle at the name of the server XXXtestor01.

Right click the name of the server XXXtestor01.

Click Review, under Configuration.

Click Add to Group.

Click Continue.

Click OK.

Click OK.

The Session VM is now configured.

Verify that the licenses are installed.

You are in the RD Licensing Manager screen.

Double-click the name of the server XXXtestor01.

You see that the 3 licenses are available but not issued.

If user U1 and or U2 log on, you will see that the licenses are issued.

Close all windows, the system is configured.

G. Connect to Remote Desktop on the Internet

1.   On your local PC, run Notepad using the Run As Administrator option.

2.   In Notepad, open the C:\Windows\System32\Drivers\Etc\Hosts. file and add the following line to the end of the file: Public _IP _Address XXXtestor01.contoso.com

After making this change, save the file and close notepad.

Note: In a production environment, hostname resolution is typically handled by the DNS servers hosting your public DNS namespace. When deploying for production purposes, make these hostname resolution updates on your DNS servers rather than in a local Hosts file.

3.   On you local PC, run: regsvr32 jscript.dll

4.   On your local PC, open Internet Explorer and browse to the following URL:

> https://XXXtestor01.contoso.com/RDWeb

> You can also use https://*the-public-url*.contoso.com/RDWeb

When asked for a certificate error page, click Continue. The certificate error page is displayed because the Quick Start configuration provisions the RDWeb web site with a self-signed certificate. In a production configuration, this self-signed certificate would be replaced in IIS Manager with a valid certification registered by a trusted certificate authority.

5.   When prompted to login to the RDWeb web site, login with CONTOSO\admin.

6.   Upon login, the remote applications defined in the default Remote Desktop Session Collection will be displayed. Calculator, Paint, etc.

CHAPTER 16 BEGIN THE INSTALLATION –

DUAL SERVERS

Set up of a Microsoft Windows Server 2012 R2 in the cloud.

This setup will use two virtual servers, one for an Active Directory Domain Controller and DNS server, and a second VM configured as a Remote Desktop Session Host, Web Access gateway, and Connection Broker. The first is dedicated to authorizing users and checking their log in and user management. The second is where the user programs and data reside. The second server can support up to 26 users at the same time. You can add servers for more users.

Microsoft charges a small monthly fee and for each user license more than two plus data transfer out of the server. If you set up a server without Active Directory, you get two licenses free.

We will:

A. Prepare the Infrastructure

B. Register a DNS Server in Windows Azure

C. Define a Virtual Network in Windows Azure

D. Configure Windows Server Active Directory in a Windows Azure VM

E. Configure Remote Desktop Session Virtualization in a Windows Azure VM

F. Install user licenses

G. Connect to Remote Desktop on the Internet

Estimated time to complete: 1 hour, 30 minutes

A: Prepare the Infrastructure

1.   Login to the Windows Azure Management Portal.

Login to the web-based Windows Azure Management Portal at http//manage.windowsazure.com.

On the blue side navigation bar at the left side, there are the options for managing Virtual Machines, Virtual Networks, Storage and Settings. You can scroll down to see all options.

2. Make a new Affinity Group.

Affinity groups group your cloud-based services together, such as Virtual Machines, Virtual Networks and Storage. Azure will keep all group services within the same data center.

a.   Select Settings from the blue side bar in the Windows Azure Management Portal.

b.   On the Settings page, select the Affinity Groups tab on the top navigation bar.

c.   Click the +ADD button on the bottom navigation bar.

d.   On the Create Affinity Group form, enter Name: Enter a unique name for your new Affinity Group, such as XXXvma01 (use your initials for XXX)

Region: Select the "South Central US" datacenter sub-region. Click the Check button to continue.

3. Make a new Storage Account.

a.   Click the +NEW button on the bottom toolbar in the Management Portal and select Data Services -> Storage -> Quick Create.

b.   Enter a unique name for your new storage account URL, such as XXXtestor01 (use your initials for XXX)

c.   Region/Affinity Group: Select the Affinity Group you created above.

d.   Geo-Replication is enabled. Your outgoing data flow will be doubled and increase cost, but it is usually worth it. Each site keeps three copies of your data.

e.   Click the CREATE STORAGE ACCOUNT check button to continue.

B: Register a DNS Server

Set the internal IP address to use for Active Directory-integrated Dynamic DNS services.

1. You are in the Management Portal.

2. Select Networks on the blue side panel.

3. Click the +NEW button located on the bottom bar and select Network Services -> Virtual Network -> Register DNS Server.

4. Enter the DNS Server Name: XXXtestdns01 and DNS Server IP Address: 10.0.0.4

5. Click the REGISTER DNS SERVER check button.

C: Create a Virtual Network

The virtual network supports Active Directory, Database and SharePoint virtual machines

1. You are in the Management Portal.

2. Select Networks on the blue side panel.

3. Click the +NEW button located on the bottom bar and select Network Services -> Virtual Network -> Quick Create.

4. Enter the Virtual Network Name: XXXtestnet01 and Address Space: 10.---.---.--- and

Maximum VM Count: 4096 [CIDR: /20].

5. For Location, select South Central US.

6. For Affinity Group, Select the Affinity Group XXXvma01 created in A.2.d. above.

7. For DNS Server, Select XXXtestdns01 created in B.4. above.

8. Click the CREATE A VIRTUAL NETWORK check button to finish.

D. Create an Active Directory in a Virtual Machine (VM)

Create a new Virtual Machine (VM) to run the Active Directory domain controller in a new Active Directory Forest.

1. You are in the Management Portal.

2. Select Virtual Machines on the blue side panel.

3. Click the +NEW button located on the bottom bar and select Compute -> Virtual Machines -> from the Gallery.

4. Select the Windows Server 2012 Datacenter from the selection list.

5. Click the right-arrow button.

6. On the Configuration page, type the Virtual Machine Name: XXXtestad01.

7. Select Tier Basic for Size A0.

8. Enter a new Local Administrator User Name: vadmin and Password: Pp123456.

9. Click the Right Arrow button to continue.

10. You are in the Virtual Machine Configuration page.

11. Accept Create a new cloud service.

12. Accept the DNS Name: XXXtestad01.cloudapp.net

13. Enter Region/Affinity Group/Virtual Network: XXXtestnet01 – that created in C.4 above.

14. For the Virtual Network Subnets, Accept: Subnet-1 (10.0.0.0/23)

15. For the Storage Account, select: XXXtestor01 – that created in A.3.b above.

16. For the Availability Set, create one name: XXXtestad

17. Click the Right Arrow button to continue.

18. Include this endpoint:

> b. HTTPS endpoint
>
> 1. Protocol = TCP
>
> 2. Public Port = 443
>
> 3. Private Port = 443

19. Click the Right Arrow button to continue.

20. You are still in the Virtual Machine Configuration page.

21. Accept the check, Install the VM Agent.

22. Click the Microsoft Antimalware box.

23. Click the check button to continue.

24. You are in the Management Portal. Wait a few minutes until the status of the Virtual Machine, named XXXtestad01, shows *running*. (And, the green squiggly stops at the bottom right corner).

25. Click on the name of the new Virtual Machine, XXXtestad01.

26. Click Dashboard.

27. You are in the Dashboard Page.

28. The Internal IP Address shown on the right side of the page should be 10.0.0.4

If it is not, click the Delete button at the bottom of the page and start again with Instruction B: above.

29. Click the Attach button on the bottom toolbar and select Attach Empty Disk.

30. Accept the file name: XXXtestad01-XXXXXX or enter: XXXtestad01-data01

31. Enter the size: 10 for 10 GB

32. Accept the Host Cache Preference: None

33. Click the Check button to continue.

34. You are in the Dashboard Page.

35. Click the Connect button located on the bottom toolbar.

36. Click Open to launch a Remote Desktop Connection to the virtual machine.

37. Enter the user name: vadmin, and password: Pp123456 selected in D.7. above.

38. You are in the Virtual Machine desktop page with the Server Manager Dashboard screen showing.

39. Do not search for printers, etc. as asked.

40. Click Local Server.

41. Click remote desktop.

42. Unclick Allow connections only from computers …

43. This will allow log on from other than computers with Windows 7 and above.

44. Click OK.

45. Click the time icon at the bottom right and set the time zone.

46. Click File and Storage Services -> Disks -> Tasks, to start the new volume wizard.

This creates a new partition on the additional data disk attached above in D.24 and format this partition as a new F: NTFS volume. This volume will be used for NTDS DIT database, log and SYS VOL folder locations.

47. Click Next.

48. Click Disk 2.

49. Click Next.

50. Click OK.

51. Click Next.

52. Accept Drive Letter F:.

53. Click Next.

54. Click Next.

55. Click Create.

56. Check Cloxe.

57. Click the upper left square to return to the Server Manager Dashboard.

58. Click Add Roles and Features.

59. Click Next.

60. Click Server Roles.

61. Click Roles.

62. Click Role-based.

63. Click Select.

64. Click install Active Directory Domain Services65. Click promote this server to a domain controller in a new forest.

66. Enter Active Directory Forest name: contoso.com   (root domain name)

CONTOSO.COM is a Microsoft server.

67. Accept the Volume Location for NTDS database, log and SYSVOL folders: F:

Wait a few minutes for the Active Directory to be installed.

68. Restart the virtual machine by clicking Start -> admin -> restart

Wait a few minutes for the restart.

We now have finished the Active Directory Virtual Machine that will authenticate all users to the system. We can use this VM for up to 25 users or add additional VMs for 25 users each.

E: Configure Remote Desktop Session Virtualization

This sets up a second Virtual Machine to run Remote Desktop Sessions. It can be faster to use one VM for Active Directory and one or more for user sessions, but more expensive. If you want to run both sessions on one VM, keep that name, XXXtestad01 for the following XXXtestrd01.

1.   You are in the Management Portal.

2.   Select Virtual Machines on the blue side panel.

3.   Click the +NEW button located on the bottom bar and select Compute -> Virtual Machines -> from the Gallery.

4.   Select the Windows Server 2012 Datacenter from the selection list.

5.   Click the right-arrow button.

6.   On the Configuration page, type the Virtual Machine Name: XXXtestrd01.

7.   Select Tier Basic for Size A0.

8.   Enter a new Local Administrator User Name: vadmin and Password: Pp123456.

9.   Click the Right Arrow button to continue.

10. You are in the Virtual Machine Configuration page.

11. Accept Create a new cloud service.

12. Accept the DNS Name: XXXtestrd01.cloudapp.net

13. Enter Region/Affinity Group/Virtual Network: XXXtestnet01 – that created in C.4 above.

14. For the Virtual Network Subnets, Accept: Subnet-1 (10.0.0.0/23)

15. For the Storage Account, select: XXXtestor01 – that created in A.3.b above.

16. For the Availability Set, create one name: XXXtestrd

17. Click the Right Arrow button to continue.

18. Include this endpoint:

      b. HTTPS endpoint

      1. Protocol = TCP

      2. Public Port = 443

      3. Private Port = 443

19. Click the Right Arrow button to continue.

20. You are still in the Virtual Machine Configuration page.

21. Accept the check, Install the VM Agent.

22. Click the Microsoft Antimalware box.

23. Click the check button to continue.

24. You are in the Management Portal. Wait a few minutes until the status of the Virtual Machine, named XXXtestad01, shows *running*. (And, the green squiggly stops at the bottom right corner).

25. Click on the name of the new Virtual Machine, XXXtestrd01.

26. Click Dashboard.

27. You are in the Dashboard Page.

28. The Internal IP Address shown on the right side of the page should be 10.0.0.5

If it is not, click the Delete button at the bottom of the page, look closely at the instructions beginning with Instruction **B:** above, and begin the Instruction **E.** again.

29. You are in the Dashboard Page. Make a note of the Public P (VIP) address for later.

30. Click the Connect button located on the bottom toolbar.

31. Click Open to launch a Remote Desktop Connection to the virtual machine.

32. Enter the user name: vadmin, and password: Pp123456 selected in D.7. above.

33. You are in the Virtual Machine desktop page with the Server Manager Dashboard screen showing.

34. Do not search for printers, etc. as asked.

35. Click Local Server.

36. Click remote desktop.

37. Unclick Allow connections only from computers …

38. This will allow log on from other than computers with Windows 7 and above.

39. Click OK.

40. Click the time icon at the bottom right and set the time zone.

42. The Server Manager screen is showing.

43. Click Local Server -> Workgroup – Change Name

44. Click Join this server to the contoso.com domain

45. Enter the user name: vadmin

46. Enter the password: Pp123456

47. You are welcomed to the domain.

48. Click to Restart.

49. Click Close.

50. Click Restart Now.

51. Login to the Windows Azure Management Portal.

52. Select Virtual Machines from the blue side bar.

53. You are in the Management Portal. Wait a few minutes until the status of the Virtual Machine, named XXXtestrd01, shows *running*. (And, the green squiggly stops at the bottom right corner).

54. Click on the name of the new Virtual Machine, XXXtestrd01.

55. You are in the Dashboard Page.

56. Click the Connect button located on the bottom toolbar.

57. Click Open to launch a Remote Desktop Connection to the virtual machine.

58. Enter the user name: contoso\admin, and password: Pp123456 selected in D.7. above.

   Note that you must use the contoso.

59. You are in the Virtual Machine desktop page with the Server Manager screen showing.

60. Click Local Server.

61. Click Remote management and make sure it is Enabled.

62. Click Dashboard.

63. Click Add roles and features.

64. Click the Next button on the Before you begin page.

65. Select Remote Desktop Services installation on the Select installation type page.

66. Click the Next button.

67. Select Quick Start.

68. Click Next.

69. Select Session based desktop deployment

70. Click Next.

71. The server XXXtestrd01 is in the Selected listbox of the Select a server page

72. Click the Next button.

73. Check Restart the destination server automatically if required, on the Confirmation page.

74. Click Deploy.

75. Wait while the deployment is made. If the server does not reset itself, restart it in the browser Management Portal window.

76. You are in the Management Portal. Wait a few minutes until the status of the Virtual Machine, named XXXtestrd01, shows *running*. (And, the green squiggly stops at the bottom right corner).

77. Click on the name of the new Virtual Machine, XXXtestrd01.

78. You are in the Dashboard Page.

79. Click the Connect button located on the bottom toolbar.

80. Click Open to launch a Remote Desktop Connection to the virtual machine.

81. Enter the user name: contoso\admin, and password: Pp123456 selected in D.7. above.

Note that you must use the contoso.

82. You are in the Virtual Machine desktop page with the Server Manager screen showing.

Add Users

1.   Click the Start icon at the bottom left of the screen. *You can also use the Start key.*

2.   Click Control Panel.

3.   Click User Accounts.

4.   Click Change account type.

5.   Click the Advanced tab at the top.

6.   Click Advanced.

7.   The lusrmgr – Local Users and Groups screen is shown.

8.   Click Action -> New User.

9.   Type in the user name: U1.

10. Type in the password: Pp123456.

11. Type in the password again in Confirm password.

12. Click Create.

13. Enter another user, U2 with password, Pp123456.

14. Close the lusmgr screen by clicking the red X at the top right.

15. Close the User Accounts screen.

16. Close the Control Panel screen.

17. You are in the Server Manager Dashboard screen.

F. Install user licenses

You can buy the user SAL licenses several ways. For this case, we assume you have a key number from a SPLA dealer and the number is 1234567890.

1. Click Remote Desktop Services.

    Click servers.

    The server XXXtestrd01 is shown.

    Right-Click the server XXXtestrd01.

    Click RD Licensing Manager.

    Right-Click the server XXXtestrd01 again that is shown as Not activated.

    Click Activate Server.

    Click Next.

    Accept Automatic.

    Click Next.

    Fill out the form with name and company information.

    Click Next.

    Enter the optional information on the form.

    Click Next.

    You are shown that the server has been activated.

    Click Next.

    You may not enter the user licenses. (SAL)

    Click Next.

The RD Licensing Manager screen is shown.

Click Action.

Click Install Licenses.

Click Next.

In the License Program drop down list, select Service Provider License Agreement.

Click Next.

Type in the agreement number. (1234567890)

Click Next.

On the Product Version drop down list, click Windows Server 2012.

On the License Type drop down list, click RDS Per User CAL.

For the number of licenses, type in 3.

Click Next.

You are show that the licenses are successfully installed.

Click Finish.

You are in the RD Licensing Manager screen.

There is a yellow triangle at the name of the server XXXtestrd01.

Right click the name of the server XXXtestrd01.

Click Review, under Configuration.

Click Add to Group.

Click Continue.

Click OK.

Click OK.

The Session VM is now configured.

Verify that the licenses are installed.

You are in the RD Licensing Manager screen.

Double-click the name of the server XXXtestrd01.

You see that the 3 licenses are available but not issued.

If user U1 and or U2 log on, you will see that the licenses are issued.

Close all windows, the system is configured.

G. Connect to Remote Desktop on the Internet

On your local PC, run Notepad using the Run As Administrator option.

2. In Notepad, open the C:\Windows\System32\Drivers\Etc\Hosts. file and add the following line to the end of the file: Public _IP _Address XXXtestrd01.contoso.com

After making this change, save the file and close notepad.

Note: In a production environment, hostname resolution is typically handled by the DNS servers hosting your public DNS namespace. When deploying for production purposes, make these hostname resolution updates on your DNS servers rather than in a local Hosts file.

3. On you local PC, run: regsvr32 jscript.dll

4. On your local PC, open Internet Explorer and browse to the following URL:

https://XXXtestrd01.contoso.com/RDWeb

You can also use https://*the-public-url*.contoso.com/RDWeb

When asked for a certificate error page, click Continue. The certificate error page is displayed because the Quick Start configuration provisions the RDWeb web site with a self-signed certificate. In a production configuration, this self-signed certificate would be replaced in IIS Manager with a valid certification registered by a trusted certificate authority.

5. When prompted to login to the RDWeb web site, login with CONTOSO\admin.

6. Upon login, the remote applications defined in the default Remote Desktop Session Collection will be displayed. Calculator, Paint, etc.

CHAPTER 17 LANGIAPPE

This is an old New Orleans term that means "something extra" like "a baker's dozen".

The site to download the free iPad program for Remote Desktop access is:

https://itunes.apple.com/us/app/microsoft-remote-desktop/id714464092?mt=8

The name of the app is Remote Desktop by Microsoft.

Enter the Gateway information:
VM1Admin.cloudapp.net:xxxxx

or whatever your number is

Enter your user name and password.

Note that when working, a keyboard icon is at the top of the page for entering text.

If you are still using a fax machine, Cut the Cord! Sign up at eFax.com. They will send all your faxen to an email address. No paper – no phone line cost – no machine.

In order to use Remote Web Access or VPN using the set up wizard, you must have an acceptable web domain with a SSL license certificate. There are three choices; Microsoft, GoDaddy, and another. I tried Microsoft in the set up wizard many times but it would not work. GoDaddy had a $4/year special on the domain but the certificate usually costs $50.

To connect VPN, you need to have a VPN router on the hardware side.

After setting it up to up and down load, I realized that we could not attach to the customer's Windows 2000 server. Because all computers must be Windows 7 or higher, the 2000 server would not work.

Check for corrections or additions at any of our web address with the foloowing suffix. For example:

www.SoftExp.net/book-15-minutes

For complements, suggestions, or complaints, please email:

Barrett Leibe

Software Express, New Orleans, mail@SoftExp.net

CHAPTER 18 SAMPLES OF ADVERTISING FOR A HOSTED SERVICE

Software Express offers a service for small businesses to replace their hardware servicer with the cloud server and to maintain a HotServer ready to be used in case of disaster or just for mobile access.

You may be in the same business or would like to begin.

Our web advertisements are at:

www.CloudHail.com

www.ServerPole.com

www.SoftExp.net

Following are some samples of our mailing:

Polygon Industries, Inc.
Increasing Productivity
P.O. Box 24096, New Orleans, LA 70184
(504)451-5721   email: mail@PolygonIndustries.com   www.ServerPole.com

Wednesday, January 07, 2015

«Coname»

Dear Sirs:

    I wrote to you twice before offering the Microsoft Azure Cloud Server as a turn-key product you can sell. However, most small businesses are not ready to trust the cloud with their system. So we are focusing on the benefits of backup and disaster prevention.

    You still retain the 35% discount, can sell under your own name and price, and there is no long term commitment. Here's the deal:

Disaster Prevention, not Recovery

There are many choices for backup and recovery. However, you business will stop while recovery takes a long time and is a headache. And, you are never sure the data is all there.

We offer a better choice: your complete system duplicated on line and available for instant use. With the data kept synchronized, there is no down time.

The cost is surprisingly affordable.
Call Now for a free trial
or look further at www.ServerPole.com

Isn't this a better alternative to simple backup?
If you have any questions, I will be glad to visit, discuss it, and show you the product. **Call me! 504-451-5721** See the info at www.ServerPole.com

    Thank you,

Yours sincerely,

Barrett Leibe

Barrett Leibe, President

Windows Azure

Microsoft
Developer Network

Plate 1

Choices in Backup and Disaster Prevention

There is now have technology that will automatically protect your computer system and data no matter what happens. It's called Cloud Computing.

Software Express, established in 1985, is specializing in this field and ready to advise you in the best choices. The costs have come down drastically. See our web site for more details of each and comparison of vendors.

1. Backup your server and PCs to a cloud storage drive. It can be set to run nightly or many times during the day. Three copies are each kept in two different locations by Microsoft. The cost is only **$5.**/month for each PC or servr.

2. The same as No. 1. But the backup can be done as each file is changed and individual files can be restored. This cost is **$10.**/month for each PC or server.

3. The same as No. 2 but it works with databases while they are open, such as SQL Server or Exchange. This cost is **$40.**/month for each PC or server.

4. The Microsoft 2012 R2 Enterprise server can be kept in the cloud ready to be used and loaded with programs and data with no delay in case of failure of your in-house server. It can be downloaded to your in-house server or used in the cloud with client PCs. This cost is **$50.**/month for each server.

5. The Microsoft 2012 R2 Enterprise server running in the cloud can be used as your primary server with access by up to 25 PCs, tablets, or smart phones. You don't need an in-house server. This cost is **$100.**/month for each server.

If you are not now using these services, call us for an appointment to talk to you about your specific system and a quote. Your IT guy should also be there.

Call Now 504-451-5721

There are about twenty companies offering these services. We will be glad to compare the values of each. Thank you.

Have a look at our web site: **CloudHail.com/bdr**

Software Express, Inc.
Increasing Productivity
P.O. Box 24096 New Orleans, LA 70471
(504)451-5721   email: mail@SoftExp.net   www.SoftExp.net/Cloud

Plate 2

New Servers for Old!!

Trade in that old piece of junk for
the Microsoft Cloud Server.

- Includes the latest system 2012 R2 Enterprise

- Includes maintenance and updates done
  by Microsoft

- Includes backup to two U.S. locations

- Work from any web device, anywhere

- Reduce you cost by HALF!

- Try it 30 days free

- also call us for automatic cloud backup
  or cloud server standby

call Barrett – 504-451-5721
Check out:
www.CloudHail.com

mail@SoftExp.net

New Servers for Old!!

Trade in that old piece of junk for
the Microsoft Cloud Server.

- Includes the latest system 2012 R2 Enterprise

- Includes maintenance and updates done by
  Microsoft

- Includes backup to two U.S. locations

- Work from any web device anywhere

- Reduce you cost by HALF!

- Try it 30 days free

- also call us for automatic cloud backup
  or cloud server standby

call Barrett – 504-451-5721
Check out:
www.CloudHail.com

mail@SoftExp.net

New Servers for Old!!

Trade in that old piece of junk for
the Microsoft Cloud Server.

- Includes the latest system 2012 R2 Enterprise

- Includes maintenance and updates done by
  Microsoft

- Includes backup to two U.S. locations

- Work from any web device anywhere

- Reduce you cost by HALF!

- Try it 30 days free

- also call us for automatic cloud backup
  or cloud server standby

call Barrett – 504-451-5721
Check out:
www.CloudHail.com

mail@SoftExp.net

New Servers for Old!!

Trade in that old piece of junk for
the Microsoft Cloud Server.

- Includes the latest system 2012 R2 Enterprise

- Includes maintenance and updates done by
  Microsoft

- Includes backup to two U.S. locations

- Work from any web device anywhere

- Reduce you cost by HALF!

- Try it 30 days free

- also call us for automatic cloud backup
  or cloud server standby

call Barrett – 504-451-5721
Check out:
www.CloudHail.com

mail@SoftExp.net

Plate 3

- Work from any web device anywhere
- $100 per month - No contract; quit or expand any time.
- Try it 30 days free
- We also do cloud backup and cloud server standby

Call Barrett at – 504-451-5721

Check out: www.CloudHail.com

Software Express, mail@SoftExp.net

New Servers for Old!!

Trade in that old piece of junk.

- Includes the latest system 2012 R2 Enterprise
- Includes maintenance and updates done by Microsoft
- Includes backup to two U.S. locations
- Work from any web device anywhere
- $100 per month - No contract; quit or expand any time
- Try it 30 days free
- We also do cloud backup and cloud server standby

Call Barrett at – 504-451-5721

Check out: www.CloudHail.com

Software Express, mail@SoftExp.net

New Servers for Old!!

Trade in that old piece of junk.

- Includes the latest system 2012 R2 Enterprise
- Includes maintenance and updates done by Microsoft
- Includes backup to two U.S. locations

- Work from any web device anywhere
- $100 per month - No contract; quit or expand any time.
- Try it 30 days free
- We also do cloud backup and cloud server standby

Call Barrett at – 504-451-5721

Check out: www.CloudHail.com

Software Express, mail@SoftExp.net

New Servers for Old!!

Trade in that old piece of junk.

- Includes the latest system 2012 R2 Enterprise
- Includes maintenance and updates done by Microsoft
- Includes backup to two U.S. locations
- Work from any web device anywhere
- $100 per month - No contract; quit or expand any time.
- Try it 30 days free
- We also do cloud backup and cloud server standby

Call Barrett at – 504-451-5721

Check out: www.CloudHail.com

Software Express, mail@SoftExp.net

Plate 4

Please let us know the following information so we can mail you a special offer. This card will save a call or visit to ask the questions.

We are using the CCiRater software:
Y / N _____

We use a file server with PCs networked:
Y / N _____

We already have a cloud backup:
Y / N _____

«coname», «add1»«Next Record»

Please let us know the following information so we can mail you a special offer. This card will save a call or visit to ask the questions.

We are using the CCiRater software:
Y / N _____

We use a file server with PCs networked:
Y / N _____

We already have a cloud backup:
Y / N _____

«coname», «add1»«Next Record»

Please let us know the following information so we can mail you a special offer. This card will save a call or visit to ask the questions.

We are using the CCiRater software:
Y / N _____

We use a file server with PCs networked:
Y / N _____

We already have a cloud backup:
Y / N _____

«coname», «add1»«Next Record»

Please let us know the following information so we can mail you a special offer. This card will save a call or visit to ask the questions.

We are using the CCiRater software:
Y / N _____

We use a file server with PCs networked:
Y / N _____

We already have a cloud backup:
Y / N _____

«coname», «add1»«Next Record»

Plate 5

Let us install your software and data as a test for you to try and see how it works. No charge.

Call now – 504-451-5721

Check out: www.SoftExp.net/Cloud

Barrett Leibe, *Software Express*, mail@SoftExp.net

Your Server is Obsolete!!

We are replacing physical file server computers with the Microsoft Cloud server. You replace all the headaches with a low monthly payment. Savings are substantial; less than half your current budget.

Benefits include triple redundant online backup, professional management, protection, security, updates, and access from anywhere by PC, tablet, or smart phone.

Let us install your software and data as a test for you to try and see how it works. No charge.

Call now – 504-451-5721

Check out: www.SoftExp.net/Cloud

Barrett Leibe, *Software Express*, mail@SoftExp.net
Your Server is Obsolete!!

We are replacing physical file server computers with the Microsoft Cloud server. You replace all the headaches with a low monthly payment. Savings are substantial; less than half your current budget.

Benefits include triple redundant online backup, professional management, protection, security, updates, and access from anywhere by PC, tablet, or smart phone.

Let us install your software and data as a test for you to try and see how it works. No charge.

Call now – 504-451-5721

Check out: www.SoftExp.net/Cloud

Barrett Leibe, *Software Express*, mail@SoftExp.net

Your Server is Obsolete!!

We are replacing physical file server computers with the Microsoft Cloud server. You replace all the headaches with a low monthly payment. Savings are substantial; less than half your current budget.

Benefits include triple redundant online backup, professional management, protection, security, updates, and access from anywhere by PC, tablet, or smart phone.

Let us install your software and data as a test for you to try and see how it works. No charge.

Call now – 504-451-5721

Check out: www.SoftExp.net/Cloud

Barrett Leibe, *Software Express*, mail@SoftExp.net

Plate 6

Software Express, Inc.
Increasing Productivity
2020 N. Causeway Blvd., Mandeville LA 70471
(504)451-5721   email: mail@SoftExp.net   www.SoftExp.net

Tuesday, July 23, 2014

«Coname»

Dear Sirs:

We are offering a product you may wish to offer to your customers. It is the Microsoft Azure Cloud Server.

As a replacement for the box in the closet, it includes the Microsoft Server 2012 R2, constant backup on the West and East Coast, disaster recovery, free updates, access from any internet device, and professional management by Microsoft. This will take a big load off your support shoulders.

There's no need to upgrade the old system; the server is up and running already and you install your programs and operate it just as if it were in the other room. Your customer will love the lack of down time. And the cost, usually $100 per month, is less than half his current cost.

Yes, you could learn to do it yourself, but we can provide and manage it immediately. You can refer your customer or prospect to us or we will provide it in your name and you set the price. Either way, you receive 35% per month.

There are many advantages that will save cost and time; full details are on our web site www.CloudMail.com.

If you have any questions, I will be glad to visit, discuss it, and show you the product. **Call me! 504-451-5721** If you need brochures, let us know. Go out and find servers to replace! See the terms at www.CloudMail.com/agency

Thank you,

Yours sincerely,

Barrett Leibe

Barrett Leibe, President

Windows Azure

Microsoft
Developer Network

Plate 7

Software Express
2020 N. Causeway Blvd., Mandeville, LA   70471

Stuff happens!! You don't need a backup,
but a duplicate server in the cloud!!

«coname»
«add1»
«city»
«state»   «zip»

Plate 8 - Envelope

Software Express, Inc.
Increasing Productivity
2020 N. Causeway Blvd., Mandeville LA 70471
(504)451-5721   email: mail@SoftExp.net   www.SoftExp.net

Tuesday, July 15, 2014

«Coname»

Dear Sirs:

You may recall that we are offering to replace existing file servers for the Microsoft Cloud Server. We would like to ask you to suggest our service to your business clients.

There are many advantages that will save cost and time; usually more than half their present cost. Our price is usually $100 per month. Full details are on our web site www.CloudMail.com.

If you would like to replace your own server, we offer a reduction of $35 per month so you can be familiar with it.

Some of the benefits are: triple backup, 99,9% uptime, disaster recovery, redundant copies on the East and West Coasts, maintenance by Microsoft experts, low cost, free updates to the latest Microsoft Server software, remote access, and low cost.

Thank you,

Yours sincerely,

Barrett Leibe

Barrett Leibe, President

Plate 9

Get $400 each !!

Help me find file servers to replace with a cloud server

Barrett Leibe, Software Express
504-451-5721   CloudHail.com

Get $400 each !!

Help me find file servers to replace with a cloud server

Barrett Leibe, Software Express
504-451-5721   CloudHail.com

Plate 10

Press Release

FOR IMMEDIATE RELEASE

SOFTWARE EXPRESS BRINGS THE CLOUD TO SMALL BUSINESS!

Mandeville, May 22, 2014, Now small business can join the Cloud Migration just as the Fortune 500 have.

Software Express, computer specialist in Mandeville, is being successful in converting file servers in businesses to the Microsoft Azure File Server in the Cloud.

There are great savings with a guaranteed cost less than half that of the physical server in house.

The cost and benefits are so great that almost all operating systems in the future will be in the Cloud instead of on boxes in the office.

Other benefits include backup in different locations, disaster recovery, automatic updates, maintenance by Microsoft itself, the latest Microsoft server operating system, and access from any internet connected PC, tablet, or smart phone. Savings also include electricity, air conditioning, and rental of space for the equipment.

Software Express was incorporated in 1985 and moved to Covington and Mandeville after Katrina. It's offices and warehouse were under 14 feet of water for three weeks in Lakeview. However, operations continued with no delay on its file servers in California and Illinois. They have sold and installed many thousands of systems in this area.

contact:
Barrett Leibe, President
2020 N. Causeway Blvd.
Mandeville, LA   70471
504-451-5721
mail@SoftExp.net
www.CloudHail.com

###

Plate 12

Software Express, Inc.
Increasing Productivity
2020 N. Causeway Blvd., Mandeville LA 70471
(504)451-5721   email: mail@SoftExp.net   www.SoftExp.net/Cloud

Tuesday, February 25, 2014

Dear Sirs:

No More Computer Headaches!!

We are replacing physical file server computers with the Microsoft Cloud server. You replace all the hardware with a low monthly payment. Savings are substantial; less than half your current budget.

We put your software on the Microsoft Server 2012 R2 in the cloud and it works just the same. You can now operate several offices and any number of users on the same server from each office or anywhere.

Benefits include triple redundant online backup, professional management by Microsoft, protection, security, updates, fail-over and access from anywhere by PC, tablet, or smart phone.

Let us install your software and data as a test for you to try and see how it works. No charge.

Call now – 504-451-5721

- No hardware to break, need service, depreciate, or update
- The latest Microsoft Enterprise 2012 R2 operating system
- Maintained 24/7 by Microsoft itself
- No licenses to buy, no patches, no maintenance
- Save electrical power, air conditioning, IT people, space
- Increase or decrease computer power or disk space as needed
- All this for $100 per month
- Optional second server across the country for automatic fail-over $50
- Install any of your software programs at no cost
- Any number of users at one time – you are the server administrator
- We are available for a group presentation

Yours sincerely,

Barrett Leibe

Barrett Leibe, President

p.s. You can get all the information on the products
on our web site: www.CloudHail.com

Plate 1

CHAPTER 19 ABOUT THE AUTHOR

Barrett Leibe started 28 retail businesses including five computer stores starting in 1977. With the first micro computers, North Star, it took three days of trying to get the video monitor to connect. All the chips had to be soldered to the logic boards and there was no application software, such as word processing or accounting. Buyers had to write their own.

The first store, Microcomputers of New Orleans, was the first business computer store between Houston and Atlanta. Sysgen Computer was the first in Germany. There were other notable firsts, too. Among them, the first language translator on the market, Translator©. the first program to hear a spoken language; translate it, and speak it in a second language; the first hard disk drive subsystems for Alpha Micro, CP/M, and IBM PC; and the first eBay store, Sell-It-Now. There are also many other projects.

His first exposure to the Windows server was with the introduction of Window NT.

The saga continues with Software Expresss offering an Azure replacement for hardware servers and the HotServer© for disaster prevention, not recovery.

Barrett is available for consultation, project management, and speaking engagements.

Barrett Leibe can be reached at:

Barrett_Leibe@compuserve.com
mail@PolygonIndustries.com

CHAPTER 20 REVISIONS AND CHANGES

February 10, 2015   So Far So Good.

February 23, 2015   So cosmetic changes.

www.ingramcontent.com/pod-product-compliance
Lightning Source LLC
La Vergne TN
LVHW012315070326
832902LV00001BA/11